SHINING A LIGHT

Shining a Light

Celebrating 40 Asian Americans and Pacific Islanders Who Changed the World

VEEDA BYBEE
ILLUSTRATED BY VICTO NGAI

 VERSIFY

An Imprint of HarperCollinsPublishers

Versify® is an imprint of HarperCollins Publishers.

Shining a Light

ISBN 978-0-35-853935-3

The artist used an iPad, Photoshop, scanned material, and analog
mixed media to create the illustrations for this book.
Typography by Sarah Nichole Kaufman
Art direction by Alison Klapthor
22 23 24 25 26 GPS 10 9 8 7 6 5 4 3 2 1

First Edition

Contents

Introduction vii

1. Yung Wing 1

2. Look Tin Eli 3

3. Tye Leung Schulze 5

4. Margaret Chung 7

5. Duke Kahanamoku 9

6. Bhagat Singh Thind 11

7. Dalip Singh Saund 13

8. Kenichi "Zeni" Zenimura 15

9. Feng-Shan Ho 17

10. Isamu Noguchi 19

11. Anna May Wong 21

12. Taro Yashima 23

13. Gyo Fujikawa 25

14. Tyrus Wong 27

15. Chien-Shiung Wu 29

16. Larry Itliong 31

17. Susan Ahn Cuddy 33

18. Grace Lee Boggs 35

19. I. M. Pei 37

20. Young-Oak Kim 39

21. Cecilia Chiang 41

22. Yuri Kochiyama 43

23. Wataru "Wat" Misaka 45

24. Daniel Inouye 47

25. Victoria "Vicki" Manalo Draves 49

26. Patsy Mink 51

27. Norman "Norm" Mineta 53

28. George Takei 55

29. Haing Ngor 57

30. Bruce Lee 59

31. Yo-Yo Ma 61

32. Maya Lin 63

33. Kalpana Chawla 65

34. Kamala Harris 67

35. Tammy Duckworth 69

36. Jerry Yang 71

37. Kristi Yamaguchi 73

38. Dwayne "the Rock" Johnson 75

39. Channapha Khamvongsa 77

40. Sunisa "Suni" Lee 79

Historical Glossary 81

Bibliography 83

Acknowledgments 97

Introduction

While walking through any Chinatown in the world, visitors may not know that the design of these urban neighborhoods was born from the creative vision of Look Tin Eli, a Chinese American businessman. College students may not realize that Patsy Mink, a Japanese American senator from Hawaii, helped write a law that gave women in the United States the right to equal opportunities in education and sports. Millions of Americans of South Asian descent may not know that they owe their citizenship to the efforts of Dalip Singh Saund, the first Asian American to serve in Congress.

During my research for this biography collection, I was inspired by these forty individuals who paved the way for all of us. I was impressed how, under great pressure, they grew to meet their hardships. I also wondered why I hadn't heard of their accomplishments when I was growing up. I didn't know that the Chinese-inspired art style of Tyrus Wong influenced not only the creation of *Bambi,* but generations of Disney artists and films. Japanese American Wat Misaka is considered the first person of color to play in the NBA, and I never saw this in the history books.

A 2021 survey from the nonprofit Leading Asian Americans to Unite for Change found that of almost three thousand responders, 42 percent couldn't name a single prominent Asian American. Another study by the University of Southern California Annenberg Inclusion Initiative tracked 1,300 top-earning films from 2007 to 2019 and found that only forty-four (3.4 percent) of these popular movies featured an Asian and Pacific Islander (API) lead or costar. Actor Dwayne Johnson starred in fourteen, one-third of all the films in the study that featured API actors in a prominent role.

The need for Asian Americans and Pacific Islanders to be represented has never been stronger. From scientists to sports superstars, artists to aerospace engineers, they have helped us better understand our world and made it safer and more magical. This collection of profiles highlights Asian Americans and Pacific Islanders who displayed courage and broke barriers to make change for the better.

These forty profiles represent just a small number of the Asian Americans and Pacific Islanders who deserve to be known. They led incredible lives, fighting for freedom and the space to be seen. I am honored to share their stories and shine a light on their courage. I hope young readers will know that they too can stand up and shape the world around them.

SHINING A LIGHT

Yung Wing | EDUCATION REFORMER

(November 17, 1828–April 21, 1912)

Because he was the youngest student at a school run by American missionaries in China, seven-year-old Yung Wing was grouped with the girls. Tired of being sheltered and longing to roam the streets like the older boys, Yung talked a few girls into joining him on a mission to steal a boat to sail back to his home village.

After a short chase, Yung's crew was caught and sent back to the school. As punishment, they had to watch as their classmates ate all the gingersnaps and oranges. The missionaries pinned a sign to Yung's shirt that read "Head of the Runaways."

Yung kept this adventurous spirit with him all his life. At age nineteen he set sail again, this time to the United States to continue his education.

Yung attended Yale College, where in 1854, he became the first ever Chinese student to graduate from an American university. While at Yale, he played football, sang in the choir, and joined the school boat club.

Yung received US citizenship while at college, but it was taken away fifty years later by the Naturalization Act of 1870. This law helped people of African descent become citizens but denied citizenship to other nonwhite groups. Nevertheless, recognizing opportunities for others, he established the Chinese Educational Mission in 1872 to bring students from China to study in the United States.

With Yung's help, 120 Chinese children received their education in the United States. Many of these students became leaders back in their homeland. Among Yung's students, Zhan Tianyou helped create China's railroad system and Tang Guo'an founded the Tsinghua School, which grew to become one of China's most prestigious universities.

Yung worked his entire life to improve education in China and the United States. Today, Yung is honored by a bronze statue on Yale's campus celebrating his pioneering efforts, and two schools bear his name, one in his hometown of Zhuhai, China, and the other in New York City.

Look Tin Eli | BUSINESSMAN

(1870–1919)

Born behind his family's store in Mendocino, California, Look Tin Eli was not allowed to attend public school because he was Chinese. Frustrated with this anti-Asian law, his father sent him back to China to receive an education when he was nine years old.

Upon his return to the United States five years later, Tin Eli was denied reentry. The Chinese Exclusion Act of 1882 was in effect, the first United States law restricting immigration based on race. The family hired an attorney to challenge this ruling and won. Tin Eli not only got back his citizenship, but also secured that right for all American-born children of Chinese descent.

As an adult, Tin Eli became a businessman and moved to San Francisco. After the 1906 San Francisco earthquake devastated Chinatown, he became a key figure in the rebuilding and preservation of this neighborhood. For years, Chinatown had faced prejudice, as many white people considered this location dirty and unsafe.

After the earthquake, local government officials thought this was an opportunity to have Chinese immigrants move to a more remote, less desirable location. Along with other Chinatown leaders, Tin Eli came up with a plan to hold on to their homes. Aware of the negative sentiment that people had for Chinatown, he hired white architects to help rebrand Chinatown. He wanted to create a place with buildings that looked like fairy palaces.

The architects used inspiration from old images mostly of religious structures, blending traditional Chinese temples with standard Western buildings. With pagoda-style roofs and bright colors, the neighborhood even offered Americanized structures, like a Chinese hospital that provided Western medicine and a YMCA in 1911.

Tin Eli's plan worked, and the reputation of his community changed. Curious visitors were fascinated by the unique buildings of the new Chinatown. This vibrant style was so successful that his vision has been replicated in cities across the world. This unique blend of architectural style is a part of Chinese American history and has inspired the colorful Chinatowns we know today.

Tye Leung Schulze | ACTIVIST

(August 24, 1887–March 10, 1972)

Chinese American Tye Leung Schulze grew up in a poor family in San Francisco's Chinatown. As a child, she was able to go to a school run by Christian missionaries, where she learned English. When she was twelve years old, her parents arranged for her to marry an older Chinese man living in Montana. While this practice was not unusual within the Chinese American community at the time, Tye wanted none of it. She refused and fled to a shelter run by the Presbyterian Mission Home. During her time at the home, Tye became a favorite student of Donaldina Cameron, a white missionary teacher and activist who helped organize raids to free Chinese women and children from slavery in California.

With her fluency in English and Chinese, Tye was asked to come with Donaldina on these raids and, as translator and interpreter, Tye assured the rescued girls that they were now safe. She wanted others to also have the freedom she found for herself.

In 1910, Tye got a job working on Angel Island, a detention center for immigrants. Tye worked as a translator and assistant matron, becoming the first Chinese woman to work for the federal government. Tye continued to use her translation talents to help the Chinese immigrants, looking out for people who were trafficked, or illegally forced to work.

While working at Angel Island, she fell in love with Charles Schulze, a white man and immigration service inspector. With biracial marriage considered illegal in California at the time, they traveled to Washington State to get married.

On May 19, 1912, a year after women won the right to vote in California, Tye became the first Chinese American woman to vote in the United States, a privilege she took very seriously.

Throughout her life, Tye continued to be an advocate and interpreter for those in the Chinese American community. She used her language skills to help fight against the social injustice Chinese Americans and Chinese immigrants faced.

Margaret Chung | PHYSICIAN

(October 2, 1889–January 5, 1959)

When Margaret Chung was a kid, she knew she wanted to work in medicine. With no toys in her house, Margaret played doctor with her food. She stitched banana peels back together, as if she was operating on a patient. One of eleven children, Margaret stepped up when her mother got sick with tuberculosis and took care of her. This had a lasting impression on Margaret, inspiring her to help others in need.

In 1911, Margaret received a scholarship to attend medical school at the University of Southern California. She was the only woman and the only nonwhite student. To better fit in, Margaret dressed like a man and started to go by the name Mike. Upon graduating in 1916, she became the first American-born Chinese physician.

Margaret began to wear women's clothes again in the 1930s, when she started one of the first Western medical clinics in San Francisco's Chinatown. Her clinic served the Chinese American community as well as many military personnel and celebrities, like actress Mary Pickford. Margaret's friendly personality earned her the nickname "Mom Chung" among the navy pilots she cared for. Margaret "adopted" over 1,500 US military personnel and many entertainment professionals, including actors John Wayne and Ronald Reagan (who later became the fortieth president of the United States).

In 1941, after the United States joined World War II, Margaret lobbied Congress to allow women to join the army and navy. Her efforts were instrumental in the establishment of the women's branch of the naval reserves, or WAVES, Women Accepted for Voluntary Emergency Service. Margaret also leaned on her Hollywood connections to organize more than seven hundred fundraisers to help support the war effort.

She was so iconic that actress Anna May Wong played a character based on Margaret in the 1939 film *King of Chinatown*. In 1943, Margaret was also immortalized in *Mom Chung and Her Fair-Haired Sons*, a comic book. A caring physician, Margaret is remembered as someone who brought people together and was not afraid to break barriers.

Duke Kahanamoku | ATHLETE

(August 24, 1890–January 22, 1968)

Descended from Hawaiian royalty, Duke Kahanamoku grew up surfing in the crystal-blue waters of Waikiki Beach. A swimmer since he was four years old, Duke entered his first race in 1911, at the age of twenty-one. During this contest in the Honolulu Harbor, Duke broke the world record for the one-hundred-yard freestyle swim by 4.6 seconds. This victory propelled him into a racing career, and being in the water became his job.

The next year, Duke set another world record during the 1912 Summer Olympics, in Stockholm. At this event, he took home gold and silver medals for swimming. In the 1920 Olympic Games in Antwerp, he broke his own world record.

Over his lifetime, Duke competed in five Olympic Games and became a famous athlete and international celebrity. After his Olympic career, Duke moved to Los Angeles, where he acted in several Hollywood movies. On the California beaches, Duke was often seen surfing on his sixteen-foot papa heʻe nalu, or surfboard.

In 1925, Duke became even more legendary when he helped save eight men from a capsized boat. He used his surfboard to swim out to the overturned vessel and to pull the men out of the ocean, one by one.

Duke's famous boards helped popularize the sport of wave riding, or surfing, which hadn't yet become commonplace. Made of koa wood and modeled after the surfboards of Hawaiian kings, the boards attracted the attention of crowds wherever he went. When Duke traveled, he would often give surfing exhibitions and show others how to ride.

The unofficial "Ambassador of Aloha," Duke would also leave his handmade wooden boards with surfers from other countries. It was his way of sharing a bit of Hawaii around the world.

In his later years, Duke was elected sheriff of Honolulu and served for thirteen consecutive terms before retiring. Though he did not live to see it, his dream of surfing being included in the Olympics was finally realized during the 2021 Tokyo Olympic Games, when surfers from all around the world competed for the gold for the first time.

Bhagat Singh Thind | WRITER

(October 3, 1892–September 15, 1967)

The first soldier to wear a turban in the US Army, Indian American Bhagat Singh Thind fought for citizenship, earning an important place in history. His case brought to light the racial injustice for those seeking to become US citizens.

Bhagat came to the United States from India when he was twenty-one. Inspired by the work of American writers Henry David Thoreau and Ralph Waldo Emerson, Bhagat left India to study in the same country as his favorite authors. As a college student in California, he joined the military to help fight in World War I. After his service, Bhagat applied for citizenship in 1918. At the time, there were laws that limited immigration. Someone who was a "free white person" and of "good character" could apply, as could those of African descent.

With no clear definition of which race one needed to be part of to be considered a "white person," Bhagat received US citizenship in the state of Washington, only to have it taken away four days later. The Bureau of Naturalization didn't agree with the decision to give him citizenship. They classified Bhagat as a Hindu, and not a white man. Bhagat was disappointed, but not willing to give up his fight.

He applied again in Oregon in 1919, receiving citizenship a year later, only to have it taken away once more. He took his case all the way to the Supreme Court, and in 1923, the court said that Bhagat was not white and was considered Asian, and thus not eligible for citizenship.

Bhagat continued to live in the United States and earned a PhD. He became a well-known writer and speaker and an advocate for the independence of India from the British Empire.

Eighteen years after he first applied for citizenship, Bhagat tried a third time. Using a law that gave citizenship to World War I veterans, he finally achieved his dream of becoming an American.

Dalip Singh Saund | POLITICIAN

(September 20, 1899–April 22, 1973)

As a young man in India, Dalip Singh Saund became interested in studying trees. He noticed the large woodlands lining the roads and saw how they offered shade for weary travelers. In India, it was considered a good deed to nurture and take care of trees for others. While waiting to be approved for a passport to America, Dalip wanted to show this kindness. He planted his own trees along the village paths, carrying water on his back to help them grow.

This love of nature followed Dalip to the United States, where he earned a doctorate degree in mathematics from the University of California. With prejudice against immigrants, it was difficult for Dalip to find work. Since he couldn't find employment with his degree, he went back to his roots and worked in farming.

For the next twenty years, Dalip cultivated the California soil. He started growing and selling lettuce. When that didn't go well, he grew and baled alfalfa hay. A law in California prohibited people of Asian descent from owning or renting land. Since he wasn't a US citizen, Dalip wasn't able to purchase his own farm. With help from a friend, Dalip farmed and leased land under an American friend's name.

While he worked the land, Dalip also fought for citizenship for himself and other Indian immigrants, becoming involved in organizations promoting the passage of naturalization laws. He helped pass the Luce–Celler Act of 1946, which gave Indian immigrants the right to become American citizens.

In 1953, Dalip started his own fertilizer business but continued to be interested in politics. A few years later, in 1956, he decided to run for Congress in California and won. This victory made him the first Asian to be elected to the US Congress and the first Sikh member in Congress. He served three terms in the House of Representatives. While in Congress, Dalip spoke out for farmers, supported civil rights, and paved the way for Asian Americans to serve in government.

Kenichi "Zeni" Zenimura

ATHLETE

(January 25, 1900–November 13, 1968)

Before World War II, Kenichi "Zeni" Zenimura was already a prominent figure in Japanese American baseball. In his hometown of Fresno, California, he played in a nisei baseball league. "Nisei" means people born in the United States with parents from Japan. He was known as "Coach" and helped bring professional white players to play in exhibition matches. Back then, Japanese Americans, like Black Americans, were not allowed to play in mainstream professional sports leagues.

After the bombing of Pearl Harbor in 1941, Zeni and his family were among the 120,000 Japanese and Japanese Americans on the West Coast who were ordered to live in incarceration camps. Zeni lost his home, but not his love of baseball. After two weeks in the hot Arizona desert where he had been relocated, Zeni came up with a plan to play ball.

With the help of his family and others in the camp, Zeni dug up a baseball field. He got a bulldozer from the camp commander and made the ground flat and level. They planted grass and built benches. Children picked up rocks to clear the field while Zeni planted and irrigated tall castor bean plants for the outfield wall. They used bags of rice for bases and old mattresses to pad the backstop. Streaks of baking flour lined the bases and foul lines.

Zeni took out ads in a local Phoenix newspaper inviting outside teams in the surrounding communities to come play. At the first baseball game at Zeni's field, six thousand people watched.

Zeni helped organize thirty-two teams of various skill levels, giving opportunities for all to participate. Other incarceration camps formed teams and were sometimes allowed to travel for competition. During this time of uncertainty, these baseball games helped bring hope to camp residents both on and off the field.

Zeni is remembered as the "Father of Japanese American Baseball." The wooden home plate from his field in the Arizona incarceration camp is on display in the National Baseball Hall of Fame.

Feng-Shan Ho | DIPLOMAT

(September 10, 1901–September 28, 1997)

As a diplomat for China, Dr. Feng-Shan Ho lived in Vienna, Austria, during a time of great upheaval. It was World War II and Germany was invading many countries in Europe, including Austria.

As German power advanced, the Jewish population scrambled to find safety. At that time, Vienna had the third largest Jewish community in Europe. Fleeing these invaded countries was difficult, as many nations would not accept Jewish refugees.

Feng-Shan thought the persecution of Jewish people was wrong and wanted to help. Working in secret and against orders from his superiors, Feng-Shan issued thousands of visas that allowed Austrian Jews to escape to Shanghai, China.

It is not certain how many people Feng-Shan assisted. While risking his career and his personal safety to help others, he received a demerit in 1939, resulting in low marks on his diplomatic record. Historians believe it was punishment for the visas he issued in disobedience to his superiors.

For over forty years, Feng-Shan was employed in diplomatic service. In Egypt, Mexico, Bolivia, and Colombia, he served as an ambassador. He eventually moved to the United States, where he retired and became a US citizen.

Though a true hero in World War II, his courageous actions went mostly unknown. Four years after he passed away, Feng-Shan's courage was recognized with the Righteous Among the Nations award from Israel's official memorial for Holocaust victims, Yad Vashem.

Isamu Noguchi | ARTIST

(November 17, 1904–December 30, 1988)

Born to a white mother and Japanese father, Isamu Noguchi never felt like he belonged anywhere. After he moved from the United States to Japan with his mother at age three, Isamu's blue eyes stood out against many of the brown eyes of his Japanese peers. He moved back to the United States at age thirteen.

Isamu found his passion in a college sculpture class. Mixing natural elements with human-made technology, he merged two worlds together. In art, he found a way to balance the struggle between his Japanese and his American cultures.

Remembering the lonely feelings he'd had on the playground in Japan, Isamu wanted to create a new type of gathering place for the children of New York City. After becoming an award-winning artist and industrial designer, he proposed the "Play Mountain" project to the New York Parks Department in 1934. Instead of the typical swings and slides, he would create an abstract playground based on a concept of "nondirective play."

His design dreams were sidelined in 1941 when the US government sent Japanese Americans on the West Coast to incarceration camps. As a resident of New York, Isamu wasn't required to move to the camps. Wanting to help his Japanese American community, Isamu volunteered to live in a camp in hopes of using his design skills to create better living conditions there. He designed plans for these sites with gardens, playgrounds, and schools. Isamu quickly realized that the temporary housing he expected operated more like prisons. His design ideas were ignored by officials, and Isamu spent six months at the Arizona camp.

After the war, Isamu went on to create many well-known works, including his famous wood-and-plate-glass coffee table, an icon of midcentury industrial design. The Noguchi Museum in New York City exhibits the world's largest collection of his work. In 2005, seventeen years after his death, Isamu's dream was finally realized when Play Mountain was completed in Sapporo, Japan.

Today, Isamu is remembered for his modern sculpture and public works of art. His lifelong desire for belonging is realized in the spaces he created where people can come together.

Anna May Wong | ACTOR

(January 3, 1905–February 3, 1961)

As a teenager, Anna May Wong would skip school to watch movies at her local Los Angeles theater and hang around film sets. She would push her way to the front of the crowd to see the actors at work and practice what she saw in front of a mirror at home.

When Anna May was fourteen, a casting call went out for Chinese women to play extras in the 1919 movie *The Red Lantern*. A family friend introduced her to the assistant director, who cast her as a girl carrying a lantern, her very first role. Anna May loved acting and continued to find work as an extra. Her parents were upset when she dropped out of high school to act full-time, but Anna May was determined. And at seventeen, Anna May landed the starring role in *The Toll of the Sea*, released in 1922. Her strong performance won public praise and her flapper fashion and bob haircut made her a style icon.

At the time, most Asian roles were played by white actors in "yellowface." They taped their eyes to change their shape, wore stereotypical clothes and makeup, and used exaggerated mannerisms to appear Asian. Sadly, Anna May lost many Asian roles to white actors. She continued pursuing lead roles without success and was usually cast in supporting roles playing Asian stereotypes. Her characters were either tragic or villainous and often died in the end. She was even asked to teach white actresses how to act more Chinese.

Frustrated with the American film industry, Anna May moved to Europe. She learned to speak German and French and earned starring roles in films in Paris, Berlin, and London. After returning to the United States, she was cast in the 1951 production of *The Gallery of Madame Liu-Tsong*, becoming the first Asian American to star in a television show. In 1960, Anna May became the first Asian American woman to be awarded a star on the Hollywood Walk of Fame.

Taro Yashima | ILLUSTRATOR AND AUTHOR

(September 21, 1908–June 30, 1994)

Jun Atsushi Iwamatsu was a successful illustrator and cartoonist in Japan. In 1933, when he spoke out against the country's leadership during World War II, he and his wife, Tomoe, were put in jail. In 1939, they left Japan for New York City to study art, leaving their small son, Mako, behind with grandparents.

In the United States Jun continued to speak out against the Japanese government. He hoped it could help make things better for the Japanese people. He and Tomoe even wrote a book about their terrible treatment in the Japanese prison.

When America went to war with Japan, Jun joined the US Army. To protect his son and family still living in Japan, he changed his name to Taro Yashima, a name commonly used in Japanese children's books. His wife changed her name to Mitsu.

Taro used his talents to help with the war effort, illustrating pro-American messages in his simple cartoon style. The US Army displayed his work in the War Information and Strategic Services offices.

After the war, Taro and Mitsu went back to Japan to bring their son, Mako, to live with them in the United States. Mako grew up to be an Academy Award–nominated film and voice actor best known for his voice work as Aku in *Samurai Jack* and Uncle Iroh in *Avatar: The Last Airbender*.

Their daughter, Momo, had been born when they lived in New York City. Taro's time with her when she was young inspired him to write and illustrate books for children. Three of his books, *Crow Boy* (1955), *Umbrella* (1958), and *Seashore Story* (1967), received the Caldecott Honor award.

Gyo Fujikawa | ILLUSTRATOR AND AUTHOR

(November 3, 1908—November 26, 1998)

Born in Berkeley, California, Gyo Fujikawa felt both out of place and ignored by her mostly white schoolmates. When she went to art school in 1926, though she was among the few women attending college at the time, Gyo again felt invisible. Yearning to develop her art, Gyo went to her ancestral homeland to learn traditional Japanese methods of woodblock printing and brush painting and to explore her connection with nature.

Gyo returned to Los Angeles and was hired by Walt Disney Studios in 1939. As the level of anti-Asian prejudice on the West Coast grew, Walt Disney sent Gyo to work in their New York City offices. Meanwhile, Gyo's family was preparing to sell their belongings to live with other Japanese Americans in the government-mandated incarceration camps. Instead of accepting the insulting prices white neighbors offered for her belongs, Gyo's mother, Yū, set them all on fire. This spark of resistance continued to burn in her daughter.

Gyo helped support her family with the money she made painting murals, creating stamps, and illustrating children's books. When she approached a publisher for her book *Babies*, they were hesitant about the illustrations, which depicted white babies alongside babies of other races. Gyo refused to remove the illustrations of diverse babies. The publisher finally gave in, and *Babies* became a best-selling children's book. It has sold over two million copies and has been translated into over twenty-two languages.

Gyo went on to create more than fifty children's books. She is remembered for her whimsical art style and her staunch advocacy for inclusion in literature.

Tyrus Wong | ARTIST

(October 25, 1910–December 30, 2016)

In 1938, Tyrus Wong was working as an artist for Walt Disney Studios. This job was not typical for Chinese Americans at the time; most had jobs at restaurants and laundries or on farms.

Tyrus had an entry-level job as an in-betweener, someone who draws repetitive images that connect key scenes. He was working in his dream field, but he was bored. When he saw that the next studio project would be an animated film of the book *Bambi,* something stirred inside of Tyrus. He thought of his mother, who he left behind in China when he came to the United States when he was nine years old. Just like Bambi, he would never see his mother again.

Tyrus spent many weekends working on hundreds of drawings for Bambi. Remembering his homeland in China, he used the landscape style of Chinese scroll paintings. When Walt Disney saw Tyrus's work, he knew this was the visual design for the film. The studio liked the simple and sensitive style. Tyrus's work captured the nature and feeling of being in a forest.

Tyrus became the lead artist for *Bambi,* and his influence paved the way for many Disney artists in years to come. Unfortunately, Tyrus was fired over an animator strike that he did not participate in. Despite his hefty contribution to *Bambi*, Tyrus was recognized only as a background artist in the film credits.

Tyrus did not give up on his art. He worked at Warner Bros. for twenty-five years as a film production illustrator. He also took jobs illustrating for greeting cards and magazines, painting murals, creating ceramics, and designing and constructing. In his retirement years, he started making beautiful kites. In 2001, Tyrus was inducted into the Walt Disney Hall of Fame, finally being recognized as one of the studio's Legends.

Chien-Shiung Wu | PHYSICIST

(May 31, 1912–February 16, 1997)

Chinese American Chien-Shiung Wu is known for her experimental contributions in nuclear physics. Often called the Queen of Nuclear Research and the First Lady of Physics, her discoveries about subatomic particles changed the study of physics.

When Chien-Shiung was a child, not many girls in China attended school. Her parents valued education and, wanting something different for their daughter, founded a school for girls. Chien-Shiung's mom went door-to-door in their small town to convince families to send their daughters there.

When Chien-Shiung had learned all she could at her parents' school, she traveled far from her village to continue her education in Suzhou. Chien-Shiung became interested in physics, the study of energy and matter, and loved it so much she would read about these subjects in the evenings on her own.

In 1936, she traveled even farther from home to pursue a PhD in physics at the University of Michigan, in the United States. Chien-Shiung became known as a careful researcher and helped run many difficult experiments. Her research on radioactive decay resulted in several important discoveries. Many of her peers thought she should have been recognized with the Nobel Prize for her contributions. Three times this award instead went to other people who had worked with Chien-Shiung. Nevertheless, her groundbreaking work cemented her place among science's great minds.

Chien-Shiung blazed a bright trail in the physical sciences, as a woman and as a Chinese American. Just like her parents, she pushed beyond gender and racial stereotypes throughout her life.

Larry Itliong | LABOR ORGANIZER

(October 25, 1913–February 8, 1977)

Larry Itliong moved from the Philippines to the United States at age fifteen, dreaming of becoming an attorney. He wanted to fight for the poor, but his own poverty made college impossible. Instead, Larry worked as a farm laborer in Alaska and along the West Coast.

Though he never became a lawyer, his desire to fight for others never left. In the 1960s, many older migrant Filipino men, or "manongs" (which affectionately means "older brother" in Ilocano) worked for California grape growers. When they came to America, laws prohibited them from voting, marrying, owning property, or starting businesses.

Manongs were paid less than other laborers, and Larry encouraged them to speak up. He organized the manongs to work together and demand improved working conditions and increased wages. When their requests were rejected, Larry and the manongs went on strike. The grape growers responded by hiring other workers.

Over the next few years, grape growers pitted Mexican and Filipino workers against each other. When the Filipino workers would strike, the growers would hire Mexican workers. When Mexican workers complained, the growers would hire Filipino workers. Larry knew they needed to band together.

In the fall of 1965, Larry and his group initiated another strike against the grape growers. This time Larry convinced Cesar Chavez, a leader among the Mexican workers, to unite with them in what would become one of the biggest labor movements in the United States. The Delano Grape Strike would last more than five years and prompt an international grape boycott. Eventually the workers prevailed, winning increased pay, better working conditions, and benefits and protections.

October 25, Larry's birthday, has been designated as Larry Itliong Day in California, in honor of his fight for farmworkers.

Susan Ahn Cuddy

(January 16, 1915–June 24, 2015)

Growing up, Susan Ahn Cuddy liked to be active. She participated in sports like basketball and field hockey, and even played professional baseball when she got older.

Susan's father, Dosan Ahn Chang-ho, was a celebrated leader in the Korean American community. When Japan took control of the Korean government in 1910, Dosan was vocal in his opposition. While visiting China, he was illegally captured by the Japanese government and taken to Japan. Arrested for his activism, Dosan died in prison.

When Japan attacked Pearl Harbor, Susan remembered her father and wanted to serve her country. She wanted to join the military, but after being rejected from officer school because of her race, she could only join as an enlisted soldier. She was the first Asian American woman to join the US Navy. Susan's athletic background led to a strong showing in basic training and Susan was finally offered a seat in officer school. Susan was the first woman aerial gunnery officer and taught pilots how to shoot down planes in air combat.

Susan would later be promoted to lieutenant in the US Navy. She worked in the intelligence division as a code breaker, and in 1947, she married fellow code breaker Frank Cuddy, a white man. As interracial marriage was outlawed in many states at the time, they were wed in a navy chapel in Washington, DC.

Working in the National Security Agency, Susan was trusted to collect information on American threats and worked on many top-secret projects. After retirement, Susan moved to Los Angeles to help run her family's restaurant.

Throughout her life, Susan continued fighting for her country and the rights and freedom of Asian Americans.

Grace Lee Boggs | ACTIVIST

(June 27, 1915–October 5, 2015)

After earning a PhD in philosophy at Bryn Mawr College in 1940, Chinese American Grace Lee Boggs had a difficult time finding a job. Discrimination was widespread; even department stores told her they didn't hire Asians. She moved to the Midwest, eventually securing employment at the University of Chicago's library.

Since Grace earned only ten dollars a week, her housing options were limited. She found free public housing in a rat-infested apartment building in a mostly Black community. Grace connected with her neighbors and saw their poor living and working conditions. She was inspired by their protests for better housing.

In 1953, Grace moved to Detroit to edit the *Correspondence*, a radical political newsletter. While there, she met James Boggs, a Black autoworker and likeminded activist, whom she married that same year. While Grace had revolutionary ideas about new systems of government, she believed that individual action could have the most impact on a community. Influenced by Dr. Martin Luther King Jr., Grace also believed in a nonviolent approach to achieve change.

Grace used her talents to write a weekly column in their Detroit newspaper discussing issues affecting her fellow residents. Grace and James started community gardens and formed organizations to distribute food, host after-school programs, and mobilize calls for reform. A philosopher at heart, Grace continually advocated for education and critical thinking as necessary to lift individuals and communities.

Grace was a force in her community, always fighting for fair and equitable treatment for people of all races, genders, identities, and socioeconomic backgrounds. Inspired by Grace's and James's service and philosophy, the Boggs Center was established in 1995 to continue their legacy of promoting community leadership.

I. M. Pei | ARCHITECT

(April 26, 1917–May 16, 2019)

Chinese American I. M. Pei is considered one of the greatest modern architects. His work can be seen in iconic buildings like the Louvre in Paris, the Bank of China Tower in Hong Kong, and the National Gallery of Art in Washington, DC.

When I. M. was nine years old, he watched the development of a new twenty-five-story hotel in Shanghai. He stared into the big, deep hole of construction and was fascinated by the process. He decided he wanted to build structures like it when he grew up.

I. M. studied in the United States, receiving his degree in architecture from the Massachusetts Institute of Technology in 1940. Concerned over a possible communist revolution in China, I. M.'s father recommended he continue to study in America. While at the Graduate School of Design at Harvard, he joined the war effort in World War II and became an expert on fusing bombs as part of the National Defense Research Committee.

I. M. believed that cities could be improved through architecture. After earning his graduate degree, he quickly found himself designing large projects like high-rise buildings. This work helped him gain the experience and resources to establish his own firm. Innovative yet classic, I. M.'s bold modern design managed to be striking while still fitting into the surrounding landscape. He used his techniques to design hotels, museums, concert halls, and academic buildings all over the world.

In 1983, I. M. won the $100,000 Pritzker Prize, the biggest honor for a living architect. I. M. remembered the opportunities given to him to study in the United States. Instead of using the money for himself, he created a scholarship fund for future Chinese architecture students to also study in America.

Young-Oak Kim

MILITARY SERVICE MEMBER

(January 29, 1919–December 29, 2005)

One of the greatest soldiers in American history, Korean American Young-Oak Kim is most known for his heroic feats in World War II. As leader of the legendary One-Hundredth Battalion, Young-Oak commanded a segregated unit made up mostly of Japanese Americans and a handful of Korean Americans. At the time, there was conflict between Japan and Korea. There were military leaders who thought Young-Oak would have trouble commanding his troop. Young-Oak insisted they were all Americans and would be united in protecting the United States.

He earned the respect of his men, and together they accomplished great things during World War II. This included one mission in which Young-Oak and another soldier captured two enemy soldiers from the German Army and took them back to the American forces. This raid secured military information that led to freeing Rome from German occupation in World War II.

After the war was over, Young-Oak continued his career in the army. He fought in the Korean War, becoming the first person of color and first Asian American to command a battalion on the battlefield. In his thirty years of military service, Young-Oak would become a colonel, and as the recipient of nineteen distinguished medals for his service, he was the most decorated Asian American soldier in the US Armed Forces.

Young-Oak was also a humanitarian. Throughout his life, he helped orphans, survivors of domestic violence, and other overlooked people. When he was a commander in Korea during the Korean War, he collected food from his soldiers to give to young Korean orphans.

After his military service, he helped start eight major nonprofits for veterans and his local community, continuing to serve his country throughout his life.

Cecilia Chiang | RESTAURATEUR

(September 18, 1920–October 28, 2020)

Born to a wealthy family in Beijing, China, Cecilia Chiang grew up in a Ming Dynasty palace with fifty-two rooms. She never had to worry about having enough food. In 1939, two years after Japan invaded China, everything changed. Cecilia's home was seized and she and her sister were forced to take a six-month journey, walking over a thousand miles, to the safety of their uncle's home.

Having settled in Sichuan, Cecilia married and had two children. When the political climate changed in China, she escaped to Tokyo with her husband. Regulations allowed them to bring only one child. They brought their daughter, May, and left two-month-old Philip, who they wouldn't see again for two years.

In Japan, Cecilia opened her first restaurant to much success. Visiting her sister a few years later in the United States, she was disappointed by the cuisine in San Francisco's Chinatown. It didn't taste like anything she ate in China. While she was helping some friends open a restaurant there, they backed out and Cecilia decided to run the place herself. At her new restaurant, the Mandarin, she would offer authentic Chinese food. Cecilia remembered the meals she grew up with and served rich and complex dishes, like Zhangcha duck, which is smoked over tea leaves, and bao bing, savory crepes filled with moo shu pork.

Cecilia wanted to give diners an upscale experience. She hung art on the walls and selected beautiful dishes, like tiny round bowls for soy sauce that looked like perfume bottles. An influential journalist wrote about the atmosphere and delicious food at the Mandarin. Soon, celebrities like the rock band Jefferson Airplane and culinary tastemakers James Beard and Chuck Williams were fans, too. Cecilia even taught cooking classes to well-known American chefs like Julia Child and Alice Waters.

Cecilia enjoyed mentoring young Chinese American chefs. Inspired by his mother's success, Cecilia's son, Philip, started P.F. Chang's, a more casual, affordable Chinese restaurant. A pioneer in the culinary world, Cecilia influenced the way we see and taste Chinese food today.

Yuri Kochiyama | ACTIVIST

(May 19, 1921–June 1, 2014)

After Japan bombed Pearl Harbor in 1941, Yuri Kochiyama's sick father was arrested as a possible risk to national security and taken to prison. He was questioned and held for two months, released only just before his death. A month later, Yuri's family, just like the 120,000 other Japanese Americans, was sent to live in one of ten incarceration camps in the United States.

Yuri lived for two years in an incarceration camp in Arkansas, far away from her former home in California. There, she spent her time volunteering, teaching Sunday school, and helping out in the dining hall, where she met her husband, Bill.

This imprisonment time instilled Yuri with a passion for civil rights. When she and Bill moved to Mississippi, Yuri was struck by the injustice she saw against Black Americans. She thought of the discrimination she experienced as a Japanese American. Yuri wanted change.

When she later moved with Bill and their six children to New York City, the Kochiyamas became active in their Harlem community. Yuri and Bill spoke up about civil and human rights and held meetings in their home. Malcom X, a prominent Black activist, came to one of their meetings and they became friends.

Malcom X inspired Yuri to fight for Asian American rights. In the 1980s, Yuri and Bill led a push for a formal government apology regarding the injustice toward Japanese Americans during World War II. Thanks to their efforts, President Ronald Reagan signed a reparations law to provide payments to those Japanese Americans who lost all they had when they were forced into camps in the 1940s.

Yuri never stopped fighting for justice. Her outspoken voice for social causes and civil rights inspired many, especially in the Asian American community.

Wataru "Wat" Misaka

ATHLETE

(December 21, 1923–November 20, 2019)

While living in Utah during World War II, Wataru "Wat" Misaka's family was spared imprisonment under the incarceration order affecting many Japanese Americans. Wat attended college at the University of Utah, where he helped the basketball team win the 1944 national championship. Wat often claimed to be from Hawaii to protect the team from prevailing anti-Japanese sentiment. Sometimes he was taken off the bench to sit somewhere else to avoid the view of racist crowds.

For Japanese Americans locked away in incarceration camps, Wat became a symbol of hope. He proved that even in dark times, a nisei, or second-generation Japanese American, could take their shot. Many Japanese Americans followed his games. When news of his championship reached the camps, the people cheered. Wat's win was a victory and inspiration to a community looking for light.

After his championship season, Wat was drafted into the US Army. Wat returned to Utah after the war and helped his team win another championship.

In 1947, Wat was once again drafted, this time by the New York Knicks, becoming the first nonwhite person to play basketball professionally. With anti-Japanese feelings rampant in the country, this historical event went uncelebrated. Even though many people did not consider Asians people of color, Wat wasn't allowed to stay at the same hotels as his teammates. Unless teammates went with him, he didn't eat at nice restaurants.

Wat only played three games with the Knicks before they released him. Instead of accepting an invitation to play with the Harlem Globetrotters, Wat returned to Utah to study engineering.

Wat's time in professional basketball was largely forgotten until 1999, when he was inducted into the Utah Sports Hall of Fame. A documentary film on his life soon followed, and in 2009, President Barack Obama honored him at the White House as the first person of color in the NBA.

Daniel Inouye | SOLDIER AND POLITICIAN

(September 7, 1924–December 17, 2012)

As he listened to the radio while he got ready for church one morning in 1941, Japanese American Daniel Inouye heard the announcer suddenly interrupt the program. He screamed repeatedly that Japan had attacked Pearl Harbor, on the southern coast of Oahu, Hawaii. Seventeen-year-old Daniel ran outside of his home in Honolulu, just ten miles to the east of the harbor, to see three Japanese planes flying over. Puffs of smoke from aircraft fire filled the sky. Daniel could see the red dot on their wings, symbolizing Japan. Running to a Red Cross station to help the wounded, Daniel knew his life had changed.

Following the attack, the US government applied "4C" classification to Japanese Americans, identifying them as "enemy aliens" and barring them from military service. This angered Daniel and many of his young peers. They petitioned the government to be allowed to serve their country. Their appeal was granted, leading to the creation of many Japanese American battalions.

In 1943, Daniel joined the 442nd Regimental Combat Team, a segregated unit of Japanese American soldiers. This brave group of soldiers would go on to become the most decorated army unit in US history, earning over four thousand Purple Hearts, four thousand Bronze Stars, and twenty-one Medals of Honor. Daniel, having suffered many injuries, including the loss of his right arm, was given the Congressional Medal of Honor, the highest award for bravery.

Daniel went to college with a desire to effect change. He earned his law degree and went into politics. When Hawaii became a state in 1959, Daniel became one of its first US congressional representatives. He was later elected to the Senate. Serving as the president pro tempore of the US Senate for two years, he became the highest-ranking Asian American in government at the time. After his death, Daniel was awarded the Presidential Medal of Freedom for a lifetime of service and dedication to his country.

Victoria "Vicki" Manalo Draves

ATHLETE

(December 31, 1924–April 11, 2010)

A San Francisco native, Filipina American Victoria "Vicki" Manalo Draves liked to take a trolley car with her family to the large city pool to watch the divers and swimmers. Afraid of the water, Vicki didn't learn to swim until she was nine or ten years old. But even with this late start, she quickly became a strong swimmer. As a teenager, Vicki was invited to join a local swim team and quickly became a top diver.

After the Pearl Harbor bombing in 1941, many people in San Francisco were distrustful and unkind to Asians. Vicki was not allowed to use some public pools. Where she was permitted to train, they would sometimes drain the water right after she finished swimming.

For competitions, Vicki was told to use her mother's maiden name, Taylor, so she would be allowed to participate. Vicki didn't feel good about hiding her Asian American identity, even if it protected her from discrimination. With support from Sammy Lee, another Asian American diver, Vicki decided to compete under her Filipino last name.

In the 1948 Summer Olympics, in London, Vicki won the gold medal in the women's three-meter springboard event, becoming the first Asian American to win gold in the Olympics. Her friend Sammy Lee also won gold, becoming the first Asian American man to bring home gold for the United States.

Staying true to her Asian American identity during a time of terrible racial discrimination took strength. Vicki was honored with induction into the International Swimming Hall of Fame in 1969 and had a park named after her in her hometown of San Francisco.

Patsy Mink | LAWYER AND POLITICIAN

(December 6, 1927–September 28, 2002)

As she grew up among the sugarcane fields on the Hawaiian island of Maui, Japanese American Patsy Mink developed a bright personality. This spirit helped fourteen-year-old Patsy to be elected as the first female student body president of her Maui high school. This victory would not be her last.

After college, Patsy applied to many medical schools, but they would not accept women as students. Undeterred, Patsy applied to law school and was one of only two women admitted to her class at the University of Chicago Law School.

While in school, Patsy met and married John Mink, a white graduate student. However, prejudice against her interracial marriage prevented her from securing a job upon graduation.

Patsy returned to Hawaii but couldn't find a law firm that would hire a young mother in an interracial marriage. So, in 1953, with the help of her family, Patsy became the first woman in the territory of Hawaii to open her own law firm.

Motivated to change these discriminatory customs, Patsy campaigned for and was elected to the Hawaii territorial legislature in 1956, and later to the Hawaii state senate. In 1964, Patsy became the first woman of color and first Asian American elected to serve in the US Congress, where she would represent Hawaii for twenty-four years.

In 1972, Patsy coauthored a groundbreaking civil rights bill prohibiting discrimination in education and requiring equal funding for women's athletics at federally funded schools. In 2002, Title IX of the Education Amendments of 1972 was renamed the Patsy Mink Equal Opportunity in Education Act in her honor.

Patsy was inducted into the National Women's Hall of Fame in 2003 and awarded the Presidential Medal of Freedom in 2014. Patsy died in 2002, but her legacy continues, helping women access equal opportunities in athletic and educational achievement.

Norman "Norm" Mineta

POLITICIAN

(November 12, 1931–May 3, 2022)

In 1971, Japanese American Norman "Norm" Mineta was elected as mayor of San Jose, California. His victory made international news. He was the first Asian American to become mayor of a major US city, and newspapers across the United States and Japan covered this historic event.

The morning after the election, Norm woke up to find a racial slur spray-painted across his garage. This hatred was not new. As a child in the 1940s, Norm grew up living in an incarceration camp with other Japanese Americans. His experiences being imprisoned and receiving racist messages like the one on his garage were what inspired Norm's political career. He wanted everyone to be treated equally. He fought for fairer laws for immigrants and others who needed protection.

Norm would go on to run for Congress ten times, each time winning the election. He served for twenty-one years and became a key figure in the passage of the Civil Liberties Act of 1988. This act provided redress, or compensation, for those Japanese Americans wrongfully imprisoned in camps during World War II.

In 2000, when he was appointed secretary of commerce, Norm became the first Asian American to serve in the presidential cabinet. In 2001, he became the secretary of transportation appointed to yet another presidential cabinet. For his service to the United States, Norm was presented with the Presidential Medal of Freedom. Norm's contributions were also recognized by Japan, which awarded him the Order of the Rising Sun.

Norm was generous with his time helping future political leaders. He gave speeches around the world about the importance of standing up for justice and equal rights for all.

George Takei | ACTOR AND ACTIVIST

(April 20, 1937–present)

Five-year-old George Takei was terrified to see two soldiers with shiny bayonets on their rifles standing at the front door of his Los Angeles home. George's family was ordered to leave their house and live in a prison camp for Japanese Americans. To ease his fears, George's parents told him they were going on vacation.

It was not a pleasant trip. George and his family traveled for days by train to an incarceration camp in Arkansas. For four years, he woke each morning to barbed-wire fences and armed guards. Their living quarters were a small horse stall.

During movie nights at the camp, George discovered the power of film. He sat in the front row, captivated by the 1939 movie *The Hunchback of Notre Dame*. George understood Quasimodo, feeling out of place and despised by the people around him. He also loved feeling transported to Paris, away from his prison in Arkansas.

When World War II ended, the Takeis returned to Los Angeles with no home or money and worked hard to rebuild a stable life. After high school, George decided to study theater at the University of California, Los Angeles, where he would earn both a bachelor's and master's degree.

George found success in Hollywood, contributing to more than forty films and television shows, but earned particular fame for his role as Hikaru Sulu in the 1960s science fiction TV series *Star Trek*. George is also a social justice activist on behalf of the LGBTQ+ community.

Remembering the power film had on him in the incarceration camps, George uses acting to help build bridges. The 2012 Broadway play *Allegiance*, which George developed and appeared in, is inspired by his childhood. Inducted into the Hollywood Walk of Fame, George was also recognized in Japan with induction into the Order of the Rising Sun for his work on Japanese-US relations.

Haing Ngor | PHYSICIAN AND ACTOR

(March 22, 1940–February 25, 1996)

Haing Ngor grew up in Cambodia, where he became a doctor and surgeon. When the communist Khmer Rouge party took control of the Cambodian government in 1975, they began executing the educated class of citizens, including doctors, teachers, and lawyers. Haing stopped practicing medicine and pretended to be a taxi driver to escape punishment.

When he was eventually discovered and imprisoned, Haing joined the hundreds of thousands of others suffering in hostile confinement. Many lost their lives, including members of Haing's family. Haing survived by eating beetles, termites, and scorpions. After four years, Haing was freed when Vietnamese forces overthrew the Khmer Rouge. He trekked four days through mountains and past hidden land mines to a refugee camp in Thailand.

In 1980, after eighteen months at the camp, Haing immigrated to the United States. Unable to resume medical practice, he found a job as a social worker in Los Angeles. While attending a wedding in 1983, Haing was spotted by a Hollywood casting director, who invited him to come in for an audition. Haing was cast in *The Killing Fields*, a 1984 movie based on the real-life experience of two journalists during the Khmer Rouge takeover of Cambodia. The movie won several awards, including the Academy Award ("Oscar") for Best Picture.

For his performance, Haing won the Oscar for Best Supporting Actor. He was the first Asian American to win the award and the second Asian actor to win an Oscar of any kind.

While pursuing a successful acting career, Haing continued to serve as a social worker, helping fellow immigrants find meaningful employment in their new home. Toward the end of his life, Haing contributed more and more of his income to fight poverty in his homeland, supporting two medical clinics and a school in Cambodia. Today, the Dr. Haing S. Ngor Foundation continues his legacy to promote the culture and welfare of Cambodian people.

Bruce Lee | MARTIAL ARTIST AND ACTOR

(November 27, 1940–July 20, 1973)

Born in San Francisco in the Year of the Dragon, the Chinese lunar calendar sign of good luck and strength, Hong Kong American Bruce Lee lived up to his nickname, Little Dragon. Moving shortly after his birth, Bruce spent his childhood in Hong Kong.

An energetic kid with a big personality, Bruce appeared in over twenty films in Hong Kong as a child. Bruce's streak of fire also got him into fights. To channel his feisty spirit and instill discipline, his parents enrolled thirteen-year-old Bruce in martial arts training.

Because Bruce seemed unable to stay out of trouble, his parents encouraged him to move to San Francisco to live with family and change his environment. When he was eighteen, Bruce returned to the United States and started college, teaching kung fu classes to pay for school. His quick, effortless style and magnetic personality made him very popular. Bruce established his own school in Oakland, California, and developed his own method of martial arts called Jeet Kune Do.

Bruce's talents were noticed by a television producer, who cast him as Kato, the sidekick to the crime-fighting lead in the short-lived television show *The Green Hornet.* After the series was canceled, Bruce struggled to find roles as an Asian actor in the United States. In 1971, Bruce went back to Hong Kong, where he wrote, directed, and starred in the successful film *The Way of the Dragon* and several others. His Hong Kong films did so well that Hollywood soon wanted him back.

In 1973, Bruce starred in *Enter the Dragon,* the first martial arts movie produced in Hollywood. Bruce choreographed the fights, performed his own stunts, and contributed to the script. It was one of the biggest films of the year and became one of the most influential action films of all time. Tragically, Bruce died from a swelling of the brain the week before the movie released. In 2004, *Enter the Dragon* was selected by the Library of Congress for preservation in the National Film Registry as a culturally significant work.

Yo-Yo Ma | MUSICIAN

(October 7, 1955–present)

Yo-Yo Ma was born in France to musician parents who wanted each of their children to learn an instrument. Not wanting to play the violin like his sister, Yeou-Cheng, Yo-Yo chose the cello. The siblings had a rigorous training schedule, sometimes waking up at four or five a.m. to practice. By age five, Yo-Yo had memorized three of Johann Sebastian Bach's solo suites, and at age seven, he was playing at the Kennedy Center in Washington, DC, for President John F. Kennedy and former president Dwight Eisenhower.

A prodigy, Yo-Yo graduated high school when he was fifteen years old and studied at the famed Juilliard School of Music in New York City. At age sixteen he began his studies at Harvard University. Wanting to broaden his horizons, he chose to major in anthropology instead of music. But with his incredible musical talent, he was destined to become one of the most famous musicians in the world.

Yo-Yo explored many types of music—from American bluegrass to Brazilian sounds to traditional Chinese melodies. He established education programs and hosted family concerts to help children develop a love of music. In 1998, Yo-Yo combined his musical and anthropological interests in creating Silkroad, a showcase for international musicians. Through this project, Yo-Yo sought to unite the world through the sharing and preserving of cultures and musical traditions.

Yo-Yo's performances, both as part of an orchestra and as a soloist, have drawn audiences and honors throughout the world. He has released more than one hundred albums and has won eighteen Grammy Awards and many international awards. For his outstanding contributions to music, Yo-Yo was honored with the National Medal of Art in 2001 and the Presidential Medal of Freedom in 2011.

Maya Lin | ARCHITECT AND ARTIST

(October 5, 1959–present)

As a girl, Chinese American Maya Lin liked building miniature towns from scraps of paper. She also loved playing in the woods near her Ohio home and watching the wildlife. These interests merged as Maya grew up. She wanted to design buildings that would blend into the landscape around them.

During her senior year at Yale University, Maya submitted an entry in a contest to design the Vietnam Veterans Memorial. Her concept differed from traditional memorials. Instead of using bronze statutes, military symbolism, or weaponry, Maya had a minimalist approach. She wanted the names of over fifty-eight thousand US soldiers who died in the Vietnam War carved into two acres of polished black granite slabs. The mirrorlike finish would cause the viewers to see themselves as they read the names of fallen and lost soldiers.

Maya's design won, and the Vietnam Veterans Memorial is considered one the most memorable landmarks in the United States. Maya's style made an impact on future memorials and has influenced many designers and architects.

As with the Vietnam Veterans Memorial, Maya wants people to have a connection with her art, not just look at it. Usually incorporating nature and landscape into art and architecture, Maya continues to design memorials, structures, buildings, and sculptures that people can immerse themselves in. Her work can be seen in many cities across the United States, like at the Museum of Chinese in America, in New York City, and at the Civil Rights Memorial, in Montgomery, Alabama.

Maya is the recipient of many prestigious awards for her contributions, including the National Medal of Arts and Presidential Medal of Freedom, which she received in 2016.

Kalpana Chawla | ASTRONAUT

(March 17, 1962–February 1, 2003)

When Kalpana Chawla was a girl, she would sleep under the stars with her mother on a charpoy, an Indian bed made of woven rope. Kalpana would look up and wonder about the sky. She was fascinated by the universe, but her mother could never answer all her questions. Even in school, Kalpana would think about space, using her free time to fold and fly paper planes.

After high school, Kalpana studied at Punjab Engineering College then went to the United States, where she eventually received a doctorate in aerospace engineering.

In 1988, Kalpana started working for the National Aeronautics and Space Administration (NASA) and became an astronaut. Her first space mission was in 1997, on the space shuttle *Columbia*. She was the first Indian and first Indian American woman to go to space.

Indians and Indian Americans alike took pride in Kalpana's achievements, watching the girl from a small town in India who grew up to fly the space shuttle. And when Kalpana would look at the stars and the galaxy, she felt like she was more than just one person belonging to one particular country; she felt a part of an entire solar system.

Kalpana was also an advocate for education, and she started sponsoring two kids from India to go to NASA's Summer Space Experience Program every year. She had a dream for all children, especially girls, to have opportunities for school and learning.

In 2003, on her second flight aboard the *Columbia*, the spacecraft exploded on the return trip to Earth, killing Kalpana and six other astronauts. Her death shook the United States, India, and the world. After her passing, Kalpana was honored by institutions in the United States and India, and she was awarded the Congressional Space Medal of Honor.

Kamala Harris | LAWYER AND POLITICIAN

(October 20, 1964–present)

Born in Oakland, California, during the civil rights movement to an Indian mother and a Black father who both shared a commitment to fighting for equality, Kamala Harris began attending protests when she was still in a stroller.

These early experiences shaped Kamala. When she was thirteen, Kamala's family lived in an apartment in Montreal. The only outdoor space was a closed-off yard that was off-limits. Kamala got the neighborhood children together and organized a protest to use this outside space, and they were soon playing soccer in the yard.

Kamala kept up her activism throughout college at Howard University. Here, she entered her first political race, campaigning for freshman class representative. After college, Kamala went on to earn a law degree from UC Hastings College of the Law in San Francisco.

In 2004, Kamala became the first female district attorney of San Francisco. In 2010, she was California's first Black and first female attorney general. While there, she started new programs to help improve the communities, like Back on Track, where first-time nonviolent drug offenders had access to life skills courses, therapy, education, and job training classes.

Kamala married attorney Doug Emhoff in 2014 and became a United States senator for California in 2017; this made her the first Indian American senator. In 2020, she became the first woman, Asian American, and Black person to become vice president of the United States.

Tammy Duckworth

SOLDIER AND POLITICIAN

(March 12, 1968–present)

In 2004, Thai American Tammy Duckworth was flying a Black Hawk helicopter in the Iraq War when she was shot down and critically injured. Close to death, Tammy lost both of her legs and almost lost her right arm. Her recovery would be one of the most challenging obstacles of her life, but Tammy knew about overcoming hardships.

Growing up in poverty in Hawaii, Tammy oversaw the family food stamps. As a teen, she would search for lost coins on the streets to buy food and sell flowers to passing cars. Her early years of struggle gave her the skills she needed to survive tough times.

It was this grit that got her through the months of long recovery from the helicopter attack. The pain and agony of her new life as a double amputee was hard, but it made her dig deep. During her year of therapy, Tammy learned how to walk, eat, bathe, and, when she fell, pull herself back up again. She prefers to use her metal titanium prosthetics over the hand-painted ones that look like legs. The steel reminds her of strength and all she's overcome.

Tammy's time serving her country wasn't finished. After retiring from the military as a lieutenant colonel, Tammy became the director of the Illinois Department of Veterans' Affairs. Working in this position, she founded the first 24-7 hotline for veterans and created programs to help them get housing and health care. Later, she worked as the assistant secretary of the US Department of Veterans Affairs. In 2016, she successfully ran to represent Illinois in the US Senate, becoming the first woman with a disability and first Thai American woman in Congress. Tammy also became the first senator to have a baby while in office.

An advocate for veterans and Asian Americans, Tammy remains outspoken in her passion to protect others. For her service to the United States, Tammy has been the recipient of many awards, including the Purple Heart, a military honor for soldiers injured in their service to the country.

Jerry Yang | ENTREPRENEUR

(November 6, 1968–present)

W hen Jerry Yang was ten years old, his family surprised him by moving from Taiwan to the United States. When he got to Los Angeles, he was overwhelmed. The only English word he knew how to say was "shoe."

In school, he was put in beginning English classes. Learning English was hard, but Jerry excelled in his math and science courses. Succeeding in these subjects enabled him to later attend Stanford University, where he received engineering degrees. Unable to find a job, he decided to return to Stanford for a PhD. Procrastinating from doing schoolwork, Jerry and his friend David Filo started working on a tool for the internet.

This project, a directory of websites organized by categories, became one of the most popular sites on the internet. Jerry and David called it Yahoo!, short for "Yet another hierarchical officious oracle." What started out as a distraction from school helped shape the World Wide Web as we know it today.

As Yahoo! grew in potential, Jerry left school to become an entrepreneur. In 1995, he cofounded Yahoo! as a company and was a member of the board of directors until 2012. Jerry is recognized as one of the most influential pioneers of internet technology and was named one of the top innovators in the world. He continues to work in technology and helps start new companies with his investment firm. Jerry also donates generously to Stanford, and in 2017, he and his wife, Akiko, gave $25 million to the Asian Art Museum in San Francisco.

Kristi Yamaguchi | ATHLETE

(July 12, 1971–present)

When Japanese American Kristi Yamaguchi was a baby, she wore casts and braces to help correct her clubfoot, a condition where legs and limbs are twisted inward. Kristi learned to walk with a metal rod between her legs that forced her feet to turn outward.

When she was six years old, Kristi started figure skating and ballet lessons as physical therapy. She loved to wear the sparkly dresses. She liked the feeling of accomplishment when she learned a new move and then mastered it. Kristi was a shy kid, and figure skating helped her feel confident. When she was on the ice, Kristi felt like she was in her haven, a safe place to express her emotions through dance. When she skated, she became a performer. She enjoyed how she could experiment with new routines and music and take on any personality on the ice.

Ice skating also made Kristi a competitor. At sixteen years old, Kristi won her first US skating championship as a pairs skater and then went on to qualify for the 1992 Olympic Games as a singles skater four years later. Despite tough competition, Kristi won the gold medal at the Olympics when she was just twenty years old.

Kristi won many championship titles, including becoming a two-time world champion. She also started a nonprofit called Always Dream, which promotes reading for underprivileged children. The program hosts summer camps for kids with disabilities and after-school programs, and helps put books into the hands of readers.

An athlete, entertainment star, sports commentator, and author, Kristi shines bright on the ice and off. In 2018, Kristi was inducted into both the US Figure Skating Hall of Fame and the World Figure Skating Hall of Fame.

Dwayne "the Rock" Johnson

WRESTLER AND ACTOR

(May 2, 1972–present)

When Dwayne Johnson received a full scholarship to the University of Miami to play football, he saw his dream coming true. After the school won the 1991 National Championship, Dwayne went on to play professionally in the Canadian Football League. He thought this would eventually lead to the NFL, but when he was cut from the team, Dwayne's hopes were dashed.

Devastated, Dwayne boarded a plane to Florida. During the ride home from the airport, Dwayne pulled out his wallet and saw that he had only seven dollars to his name. It felt like he'd hit bottom.

Dwayne kept thinking about his college friends making millions in the NFL while he was unemployed. He knew he had to come up with a new plan. With football behind him, Dwayne decided to pursue a sport he'd known all his life: wrestling.

Dwayne's Samoan grandfather was Peter Maivia, also known as "High Chief," his professional wrestling name. Dwayne's Black father, Rocky Johnson, was another WWE wrestler. Dwayne focused his energy on training, and in 1996, he made his debut in the professional wrestling ring. In homage to his grandfather and father, Dwayne went by the name Rocky Maivia. He quickly became a popular figure and soon would be known as "the Rock." During his eight years in the WWE, Dwayne won every major wrestling award. He is regarded as one of the greatest WWE wrestlers of all time.

At the height of his wrestling career, Dwayne began to pursue acting, capturing the lead role in the 2002 film *The Scorpion King*. In 2012, he cofounded Seven Bucks Productions, an entertainment company named after the amount of money he had after he was cut from football and had no place else to go. Having starred in several movies, including the *Jumanji* series and the *Fast & Furious* films, Dwayne is now one of the highest-paid actors in Hollywood.

Channapha Khamvongsa

ACTIVIST

(June 19, 1973–present)

When Channapha Khamvongsa was working in Washington, DC, at a philanthropy foundation, she was given a binder of drawings that would change her life. A man named John Cavanagh knew of Channapha's Lao American ancestry. He knew her family came over to the United States as refugees fleeing Laos during a time of war. He thought she would be interested in seeing sketches collected from a Lao refugee camp from 1970 to 1971.

These drawings were made with crayons, pens, pencils, and markers. Some of the art showed the experiences of survivors who were injured when they came across unexploded ordnance, or bombs, that were dropped by the US military onto Laos during the Vietnam War.

Channapha was shocked to discover this history. She learned that there were 270 million cluster bombs, grenades, bullets, and mines dropped onto a country the size of Minnesota. An estimated eighty million of these bombs didn't detonate. Decades later, unsuspecting people, many of whom are children, are still finding these explosives. Over twenty thousand people have been injured or killed from these bombs left behind by the war.

Channapha decided she needed to help. She spent the next twelve years raising awareness of this issue, and in 2016, President Obama became the first US president to visit Laos. During his time there, he expressed regret for the situation and said the United States would increase funding to help clear the bombs.

In 2017, Congress approved $90 million to aid with the security and safety of the Lao villagers affected. By speaking out to Congress and founding the nonprofit organization Legacies of War, Channapha has been a voice for the removal of ordnance and for education about the continued effects of these bombings in Laos.

Sunisa "Suni" Lee | ATHLETE

(March 9, 2003–present)

Intrigued by YouTube videos of Olympic gymnasts, six-year-old Sunisa "Suni" Lee wanted to try the sport herself. In their home in Saint Paul, Minnesota, her father, John, taught Suni how to do backflips off her bed. Soon she was doing flips in her backyard, in the park, and everywhere else. Since her family was unable to afford a balance beam, John built one in the backyard out of plywood and a spare mattress.

Her family signed Suni up for gymnastics classes, where her skill was immediately noticed. To help with the cost of training, Suni's parents took on three or four jobs and even held fundraisers for additional money. Many in Saint Paul's Hmong American community contributed and cheered her on.

In 2019, Suni's dad fell off a ladder days before the national championships. He suffered broken bones and a spinal injury that paralyzed him from the waist down. Suni was devastated, but John persuaded her to go to the competition. From his hospital bed, he watched Suni take the gold in the uneven bars and place second in the all-around, an event that requires precision in the vault, floor exercise, uneven bars, and beam.

Suni's Olympic debut was delayed by the COVID-19 pandemic as the 2020 Tokyo Olympic Games were postponed. During this time, she also lost a beloved aunt and uncle to the virus.

In 2021, the Tokyo Olympic Games resumed. Suni became the first Hmong American Olympian and the first Asian American to win gold for the all-around women's gymnastics competition. She also took home a bronze medal in the uneven bars and a silver medal with her team.

Her victory was a triumph for the Hmong American community, especially those who supported her throughout her athletic journey. For her achievements and inspiring effect on her community, the state of Minnesota and city of Saint Paul declared June 30, 2021, as Sunisa Lee Day.

Historical Glossary

1. **Missionary schools**—Primarily founded and run by Christian missionaries, these institutions were used to promote charity, introduce Western religion, and teach standard school subjects.

2. **Chinese Exclusion Act of 1882**—The first law to control immigration based on race, this act restricted Chinese people from moving to the United States. It was also used to remove many Chinese American citizens who were already living in the United States.

3. **Japanese occupation of Korea**—From 1910 until the end of World War II in 1945, Korea was under Japanese rule. During this occupation, Japan sought to replace Korean language, history, and culture.

4. **World War II**—A global war involving over thirty countries that started with the Nazi German takeover of Poland in 1939. The most destructive conflict in human history, with over fifty million soldiers and civilians killed, the war lasted for six years, until Germany and Japan were defeated in 1945.

5. **Japanese invasion of China**—Japan invaded Northern China in 1931 and maintained control over this region of Asia until China's strengthened forces took the territory back in 1945.

6. **Pearl Harbor**—A US military base located near Honolulu, Hawaii. Japanese aircraft attacked the base by surprise on December 7, 1941. The devastation led the United States to declare war on Japan and enter World War II.

7. **Incarceration camps during World War II**—In 1942 after the attack on Pearl Harbor, the United States established a total of ten prison camps, forcing over 120,000 people of Japanese descent to leave their homes and take residence there for the remainder of the war.

8. **The Korean War**—A civil war from 1950 to 1953 between the Democratic People's Republic of Korea (known today as North Korea) and the Republic of Korea to the south.

9. **Civil Rights Act of 1964**—A civil rights and labor law banning employment discrimination on the basis of race, color, religion, sex, or national origin, and also ending segregation in public spaces and schools.

10. **Amendments to the Immigration and Nationality Act (1965)**—This legislation removed limitations on the numbers of immigrants allowed into the United States from certain nations of origin. This law allowed immigrant families to reunite and attracted skilled laborers to the United States.

11. **Khmer Rouge seizure of the Cambodian government**—From 1975 to 1979, the Communist Party of Kampuchea, also known as the Khmer Rouge, took over the Southeast Asian country of Cambodia. During their brutal rule, the lives of over two million people were taken in one of the worst crimes against humanity.

12. **The Vietnam War**—Officially a conflict between North Vietnam and South Vietnam, this war from 1955 to 1975 also involved the Southeast Asian countries of Laos and Cambodia. In an attempt to stop supplies reaching Vietnam, the allied forces (including the United States) dropped two million tons of bombs on Laos, making it the most bombed country per capita in the world.

Bibliography

1. Yung Wing

Chinese American: Exclusion/Inclusion. "Yung Wing." New-York Historical Society. (chinese american.nyhistory.org/exhibition-highlights/yung-wing, accessed July 20, 2020)

Connecticut History. "Yung Wing." (connecticuthistory.org/people/yung-wing, accessed Aug. 17, 2020)

Council on East Asian Studies. "Yung Wing." Yale MacMillian Center. (ceas.yale.edu/yung-wing, accessed May 29, 2021)

Wing, Yung. *My Life in China and America.* New York, 1909; Project Gutenberg, 2020. (www.gutenberg.org/files/54635/54635-h/54635-h.htm)

2. Look Tin Eli

Davis, Chelsea. "Pagodas and Dragon Gates." Aired Dec. 8, 2015, on *99% Invisible.* Podcast, 27:30. (99percentinvisible.org/episode/pagodas-dragon-gates)

Kelley House Museum. "The Story of Look Tin Eli." (www.arcgis.com/apps/Cascade/index.html?appid=eb94fa453da84b6493e9e6e035675d9a, accessed Nov. 20, 2020)

Schwartz, Karen. "The Photographs That Revealed a Family Hero." History. (www.history.com/the-promised-land/the-chinese-photographs.html, accessed Feb. 26, 2021)

3. Tye Leung Schulze

Angel Island Immigration Station Foundation. "Tye Leung and Charles Schulze, an Untold Angel Island Love Story." (www.immigrant-voices.aiisf.org/stories-by-author/988-tye-leung-and-charles-schulze-an-untold-angel-island-love-story, accessed Sept. 2, 2020)

Diamond, Anna. "The Women Who Waged War against Sex Trafficking in San Francisco." *Smithsonian Magazine,* May 8, 2019. (www.smithsonianmag.com/history/women-banded-together-fight-slavery-san-francisco-180972113)

Dun, Lia. "Interpreter, Voter, and Pinball Aficionado." Angel Island Immigration Station Foundation. (www.immigrant-voices.aiisf.org/stories-by-author/807-interpreter-voter-and-pinball-aficionado, accessed July 20, 2020)

National Park Service. "Tye Leung Schulze." (www.nps.gov/people/tye-leung-schulze.htm, accessed Aug. 17, 2020)

Unladylike Productions, LLC. "Tye Leung Schulze." UNLADYLIKE2020. Video, 10:18. (unladylike2020.com/profile/tye-leung-schulze, accessed Aug. 17, 2020)

4. Margaret Chung

American Masters PBS Series. "The First American-Born Chinese Woman Doctor." Video, 10:18. (www.pbs.org/wnet/americanmasters/first-american-born-chinese-woman-doctor-ysk233/14464, accessed Sept. 4, 2020)

National Park Service. "Dr. Margaret 'Mom' Chung." Sept. 16, 2020. (www.nps.gov/people/dr-margaret-mom-chung.htm)

Women's Museum of California. "First in Their Field: Margaret Chung." July 25, 2018. (womensmuseum.wordpress.com/2018/07/25/first-in-their-field-margaret-chung)

5. Duke Kahanamoku

Beschloss, Michael. "Duke of Hawaii: A Swimmer and Surfer Who Straddled Two Cultures." *New York Times*, Aug. 23, 2014. (www.nytimes.com/2014/08/23/upshot/duke-of-hawaii-a-swimmer-and-surfer-who-straddled-two-cultures.html)

Plucinska, Joanna. "New Google Doodle Honors Duke Kahanamoku, the Father of Surfing." *Time*, Aug. 23, 2015. (time.com/4007604/duke-kahanamoku)

Library of Congress. "Duke Kahanamoku." (www.loc.gov/item/today-in-history/august-11, accessed Aug. 3, 2020)

6. Bhagat Singh Thind

Deslippe, Philip. "Bhagat Singh Thind in Jail." *South Asian American Digital Archive.* Feb. 19, 2018. (www.saada.org/tides/article/bhagat-singh-thind-in-jail)

Dr. Bhagat Singh Thind. "His Life's Work." (www.bhagatsinghthind.com/about/his-lifes-work, accessed Aug. 4, 2020)

Echoes of Freedom: South Asian Pioneers in California, 1899–1965. "Chapter 10: US vs. Bhagat Singh Thind." Berkeley Library. July 6, 2020. (guides.lib.berkeley.edu/echoes-of-freedom/bhagat-singh-thind)

7. Dalip Singh Saund

Chandler, Stacey Flores. "Asian/Pacific American Heritage Month: Dalip Singh Saund." National Archives. May 15, 2020. (jfk.blogs.archives.gov/2020/05/15/dalip-singh-saund)

History, Art & Archives. "Dalip Singh Saund." United States House of Representatives. (history.house.gov/Collection/Detail/29982, accessed Oct. 15, 2020)

Patterson, Tom. "Triumph and Tragedy of Dalip Saund." PBS. Oct. 15, 2020. (www.pbs.org/rootsinthesand/i_dalip1.html)

Pew Research Center. "Breaking Barriers: Congressman Dalip Singh Saund." Dec. 19, 2008. (www.pewforum.org/2008/12/19/breaking-barriers-congressman-dalip-singh-saund)

8. Kenichi "Zeni" Zenimura

Coffey, Alex. "A Field of Dreams in the Arizona Desert." National Baseball Hall of Fame. (baseballhall.org/discover/a-field-of-dreams-in-the-arizona-desert, accessed Nov. 20, 2020)

Davis, David. "A Field in the Desert That Felt Like Home: An Unlikely Hero Sustained Hope for Japanese-Americans Interned in World War II." *Sports Illustrated*, Nov. 16, 1998. (vault.si.com/vault/1998/11/16/a-field-in-the-desert-that-felt-like-home-an-unlikely-hero-sustained-hope-for-japanese-americans-interned-in-world-war-ii)

Tsutsui, Laura. "Even Behind Barbed Wire, Fresno Baseball Legend Kenichi Zenimura Broke Barriers." KVPR/NPR for Central California. Feb. 7, 2020. (www.kvpr.org/

community/2020-02-07/even-behind-barbed-wire-fresno-baseball-legend-kenichi-zenimura-broke-barriers#stream/0)

9. Feng-Shan Ho

CBD College. "Dr. Feng Shan Ho: Unknown Hero." May 11, 2017. (www.cbd.edu/2017/05/11/dr-feng-shan-ho)

Gordon, David B. "A Tale of Two Diplomats: Ho Fengshan, Sugihara Chiune, and Jewish Efforts to Flee Nazi Europe." *Education about Asia*, vol. 20, no. 2 (Fall 2015). (www.asianstudies.org/publications/eaa/archives/a-tale-of-two-diplomats-ho-fengshan-sugihara-chiune-and-jewish-efforts-to-flee-nazi-europe)

Kofman, Shlomi. "To the Diplomats Who Risked Their Lives to Save Jews, We Say Thank You." The Jewish News of Northern California. Jan. 22, 2021. (jweekly.com/2021/01/22/to-the-diplomats-who-risked-their-lives-to-save-jews-we-say-thank-you)

10. Isamu Noguchi

Li, Jennifer. "Isamu Noguchi Was Thinking about Public Spaces All the Time." *Architectural Digest*, Aug. 21, 2019. (www.architecturaldigest.com/story/isamu-noguchi-was-thinking-about-public-spaces-all-the-time)

Marchese, Kieron. "Isamu Noguchi Museum Launches Online Archive of 60,000 Unique Pieces." *Designboom*. Nov. 27, 2019. (www.designboom.com/design/isamu-noguchi-museum-launches-online-archive-11-27-2019)

Noguchi. "Biography." (www.noguchi.org/isamu-noguchi/biography/biography, accessed Nov. 15, 2021)

Roach, Wiley Jackson. "Play Mountain." Aired Apr. 23, 2019, on *99% Invisible*. Podcast, 37:16. (99percentinvisible.org/episode/play-mountain)

11. Anna May Wong

Alexander, Kerri Lee. "Anna May Wong." National Women's History Museum. (www.womenshistory.org/education-resources/biographies/anna-may-wong, accessed Nov. 21, 2020)

Desta, Yohana. "*Hollywood*: The True Story of Anna May Wong and *The Good Earth*." *Vanity Fair*, May 1, 2020. (www.vanityfair.com/hollywood/2020/05/hollywood-ryan-murphy-anna-may-wong)

Google Doodle. "Celebrating Anna May Wong." Jan. 20, 2020. (www.google.com/doodles/celebrating-anna-may-wong)

Holcombe, Madeline. "Google Doodle Celebrates Anna May Wong Nearly 100 Years after Her First Leading Role. Here's Why She's in Focus." CNN. Jan. 22, 2020. (www.cnn.com/2020/01/22/us/anna-may-wong-google-trnd/index.html)

12. Taro Yashima

Cormaci, Carol. "La Cañada History: Artist Taro Yashima a Paradise Canyon Elementary Guest in July 1959." *Los Angeles Times*, July 22, 2019. (www.latimes.com/socal/la-canada-valley-sun/entertainment/story/2019-07-22/la-canada-history-artist-taro-yashima-paradise-canyon-elementary-guest)

Oliver, Myrna. "Obituaries: Taro Yashima; Artist, Author Aided U.S. in World War II." *Los Angeles Times*, July 6, 1994. (www.latimes.com/archives/la-xpm-1994-07-06-me-12261-story.html)

USM de Grummond Collection. Taro Yashima Papers. (www.lib.usm.edu/legacy/degrum/public_html/html/research/findaids/yashima.htm, accessed Aug. 3, 2020)

13. Gyo Fujikawa

Amidi, Amid. "Discover the Pioneering Japanese-American Animation Artists of the Golden Age." Cartoon Brew. Dec. 4, 2008. (www.cartoonbrew.com/classic/japanese-american-animation-artists-of-the-golden-age-9375.html)

Larson, Sarah. "How Gyo Fujikawa Drew Freedom in Children's Books." *New Yorker*, June 21, 2019. (www.newyorker.com/books/page-turner/how-gyo-fujikawa-drew-freedom-in-childrens-books)

McDowell, Edwin. "Gyo Fujikawa, 90, Creator of Children's Books." *New York Times*, Dec. 7, 1998. (www.nytimes.com/1998/12/07/arts/gyo-fujikawa-90-creator-of-children-s-books.html)

14. Tyrus Wong

Chang, Rosalind. "A Profile of Tyrus Wong." Angel Island Immigration Station Foundation. (www.immigrant-voices.aiisf.org/stories-by-author/587-wong-tyrus-3, accessed Oct. 4, 2020)

Ho, Melanie. "The Chinese Artist Who Drew Disney's Bambi: A Look at the Life of the Immigrant behind the Illustrations." *South China Morning Post*, Jan. 16, 2020. (www.scmp.com/lifestyle/arts-culture/article/3046305/chinese-artist-who-drew-disneys-bambi-look-life-immigrant)

NBC News. "Tyrus Wong, Pioneer 'Bambi' Artist, Dies at 106." Dec. 30, 2016. (www.nbcnews.com/news/asian-america/tyrus-wong-pioneer-bambi-artist-dies-106-n701706)

15. Chien-Shiung Wu

Girl Museum. "STEM Girls: Chien Shiung Wu." Apr. 1, 2015. (www.girlmuseum.org/stem-girls-chien-shiung-wu)

National Park Service. "Dr. Chien-Shiung Wu, the First Lady of Physics." (www.nps.gov/people/dr-chien-shiung-wu-the-first-lady-of-physics.htm, accessed Nov. 2020)

Physics Today. "Chien-Shiung Wu." May 31, 2016. (physicstoday.scitation.org/do/10.1063/pt.5.031232/full)

16. Larry Itliong

Cowan, Jill. "A Leader of Farmworkers, and Filipinos' Place in American History." *New York Times,* Oct. 21, 2019. (www.nytimes.com/2019/10/21/us/larry-itliong-farmworkers.html)

Morehouse, Lisa. "Grapes of Wrath: The Forgotten Filipinos Who Led a Farmworker Revolution." NPR. Sept. 19, 2015. (www.npr.org/sections/thesalt/2015/09/16/440861458/grapes-of-wrath-the-forgotten-filipinos-who-led-a-farmworker-revolution)

Romasanta, Gayle. "Why It Is Important to Know the Story of Filipino-American Larry Itliong." *Smithsonian Magazine,* July 24, 2019. (www.smithsonianmag.com/smithsonian-institution/why-it-is-important-know-story-filipino-american-larry-itliong-180972696)

17. Susan Ahn Cuddy

Kim, Sung. "Susan Ahn Cuddy: Asian American Trailblazer." Los Angeles Public Library. May 6, 2020. (lapl.org/collections-resources/blogs/lapl/susan-ahn-cuddy-asian-american-trailblazer)

Susan Ahn Cuddy. "Susan Ahn Cuddy—A True Role Model." (www.susanahncuddy.com, accessed Jan. 10, 2021)

Warren, Mia, and Emma Bowman. "Their 'Tough' Mom Was Also the Navy's 1st Asian American Woman Officer." NPR. Aug. 17, 2019. (www.npr.org/2019/08/17/751418920/their-tough-mom-was-also-the-navy-s-1st-asian-american-woman-officer)

18. Grace Lee Boggs

Chow, Kat. "Grace Lee Boggs, Activist and American Revolutionary, Turns 100." NPR. June 27, 2015. (www.npr.org/sections/codeswitch/2015/06/27/417175523/grace-lee-boggs-activist-and-american-revolutionary-turns-100)

Li, Sara. "Who Was Grace Lee Boggs, the Asian American Labor Organizer and Writer?" *Teen Vogue*, May 27, 2020. (www.teenvogue.com/story/grace-lee-boggs-asian-american-labor-organizer-writer-og-history)

Rosen, Zak. "Remembering Detroit's Grace Lee Boggs." Michigan Radio. Oct. 5, 2015. (www.michiganradio.org/post/remembering-detroits-grace-lee-boggs)

19. I. M. Pei

Goldberger, Paul. "I.M. Pei, Master Architect Whose Buildings Dazzled the World, Dies at 102." *New York Times*, May 16, 2019. (www.nytimes.com/2019/05/16/obituaries/im-pei-dead.html)

Ingalls, Julia. "'The Element of Time': Celebrating a Century of I.M. Pei." Archinect. Apr. 26, 2017. (archinect.com/features/article/150003981/the-element-of-time-celebrating-a-century-of-i-m-pei)

World Architecture Community. "The 12 Most Significant Projects of I.M. Pei." May 17, 2019. (worldarchitecture.org/article-links/ecpvn/the-12-most-significant-projects-of-i-m-pei.html)

20. Young-Oak Kim

100th Infantry Battalion Veterans Education Center. "Young Oak Kim." (www.100th battalion.org/history/veterans/officers/young-oak-kim, accessed Apr. 12, 2021)

National Museum of the United States Army. "Young Oak Kim." (www.thenmusa.org/ biographies/young-oak-kim, accessed Sept. 3, 2021)

Young Oak Kim Center for Korean American Studies. "Who Is Young Oak Kim." University of California, Riverside. (yokcenter.ucr.edu/youngoakkim.php, accessed Oct. 11, 2021)

21. Cecilia Chiang

Bauer, Michael. "Cecilia Chiang." *Saveur*, Jan. 23, 2013. (www.saveur.com/article/Travels/ Saveur-100-Cecilia-Chiang)

Duffett, Becky, and Eve Batey. "Bay Area Luminaries Share Memories of Cecilia Chiang, the Life of the Party." Eater San Francisco. Oct. 30, 2020. (sf.eater.com/21541121/ cecilia-chiang-belinda-leong-george-chen-mourad-lahlou)

PBS. "Q&A with Cecilia Chiang of the Mandarin Restaurant." (www.pbs.org/food/ features/qa-cecilia-chiang-mandarin-restaurant, accessed Dec. 15, 2020)

22. Yuri Kochiyama

California State University. "Yuri Kochiyama." (www.calstate.edu/impact-of-the-csu/ alumni/Honorary-Degrees/Pages/yuri-kochiyama.aspx, accessed May 5, 2021)

Momo. "Yuri Kochiyama (1921–2014)." Center for Asian American Media. June 2, 2014. (caamedia.org/blog/2014/06/02/yuri-kochiyama-1921-2014)

Wang, Hansi Lo. "Yuri Kochiyama, Activist and Former World War II Internee, Dies at 93." NPR. June 2, 2014. (www.npr.org/sections/codeswitch/2014/06/02/318072652/ japanese-american-activist-and-malcolm-x-ally-dies-at-93)

23. Wataru "Wat" Misaka

Chappell, Bill. "Pro Basketball's First Asian-American Player Looks at Lin, and Applauds." NPR. Feb. 14, 2012. (www.npr.org/sections/thetwo-way/2012/02/15/146888834/ pro-basketballs-first-asian-american-player-looks-at-lin-and-applauds)

Kragthorpe, Kurt. "Utah's Wat Misaka, Asian-American Pioneer in Both College and

Pro Basketball, Dies at 95." *Salt Lake Tribune*, Nov. 21, 2019. (www.sltrib.com/sports/
utah-utes/2019/11/21/utahs-wat-misaka-asian)

Smith, Harrison. "Wat Misaka, Who Broke Pro Basketball's Color Barrier, Dies at
95." *Washington Post*, Nov. 24, 2019. (www.washingtonpost.com/local/obituaries/
wat-misaka-who-broke-pro-basketballs-color-barrier-dies-at-95/2019/11/24/
b5e3c242-0ed5-11ea-bf62-eadd5d11f559_story.html)

24. Daniel Inouye

Hersh, Seymour M. "Daniel Inouye's Conscience." *New Yorker*, Dec. 18, 2012. (www
.newyorker.com/news/news-desk/daniel-inouyes-conscience)

McFadden, Robert D. "Daniel Inouye, Hawaii's Quiet Voice of Conscience in Senate,
Dies at 88." *New York Times*, Dec. 17, 2012. (www.nytimes.com/2012/12/18/us/
daniel-inouye-hawaiis-quiet-voice-of-conscience-in-senate-dies-at-88.html)

Sanefuji, Noriko. "Aloha and Farewell to the Honorable Senator Daniel K. Inouye."
National Museum of American History. Dec. 21, 2012. (americanhistory.si.edu/
blog/2012/12/aloha-and-farewell-to-the-honorable-senator-daniel-k-inouye.html)

25. Victoria "Vicky" Manalo Draves

Francisco, Eric. "Why Vicki Draves' Story Is So Powerful, 72 Years Later." Inverse. (www.
inverse.com/culture/vicki-draves, accessed Oct. 2, 2020)

Kortemeier, Todd. "Diver Vicki Draves Honored with Google Doodle on Olympic
Anniversary." Team USA. Aug. 3, 2020. (www.teamusa.org/News/2020/August/03/
Diver-Vicki-Draves-Honored-With-Google-Doodle-On-Olympic-Anniversary)

Peng, Sheng. "The Golden Friendship between the Two First Asian American Olympic
Champions." NBC News. May 22, 2019. (www.nbcnews.com/news/asian-america/
golden-friendship-between-two-first-asian-american-olympic-champions-n1006191)

26. Patsy Mink

History, Art & Archives. "Mink, Pasty Takemoto." United States House of Representatives. Nov. 11, 2020. (history.house.gov/People/detail/18329)

Lang, Cady. "1972: Patsy Takemoto Mink." *Time*, Mar. 5, 2020. (time.com/5793641/

patsy-takemoto-mink-100-women-of-the-year)

National Park Service. "Patsy Mink." (www.nps.gov/people/patsy-mink.htm, accessed Nov. 13, 2020.

27. Norman "Norm" Mineta

History Art & Archives. "Mineta, Norman Y." United States House of Representatives. (history.house.gov/People/Detail/18323, accessed Nov. 2, 2020)

National Portrait Gallery. "Now on View: Portrait of Norman Mineta." Smithsonian Institution. July 28, 2010. (npg.si.edu/blog/now-on-view-portrait-norman-mineta)

PBS. *Norman Mineta and His Legacy: An American Story.* Video. (www.pbs.org/show/norman-mineta-and-his-legacy-american-story, accessed Aug. 1, 2020)

28. George Takei

Hewitt, Alison. "Q&A: George Takei on Activism, Humor and Social Media." UCLA Newsroom. June 11, 2020. (newsroom.ucla.edu/stories/q-a-george-takei-on-activism-humor-and-social-media)

National Portrait Gallery. "George Takei." Smithsonian Institution. (npg.si.edu/object/npg_NPG.2015.114, accessed Nov. 22, 2020)

Takei, George. *They Called Us Enemy.* Marietta, GA: Top Shelf Productions, 2019.

29. Haing Ngor

Baker, KC. "*The Killing Fields* Actor Killed in 1996 L.A. Shooting Told World about Brutal Khmer Rouge Regime." *People*, Dec. 2, 2019. (people.com/crime/haing-ngor-killing-fields-actor-murdered-los-angeles-spoke-out-cambodia)

Center for Asian American Media. "The Killing Fields of Dr. Haing S. Ngor." (caamedia .org/killing-fields-of-dr-haing-s-ngor, accessed Nov. 20, 2021)

Sun, Rebecca. "Tragedy Behind the 'Killing Fields' Star Who Won a Supporting Actor Oscar." *Hollywood Reporter*, Feb. 24, 2016. (www.hollywoodreporter.com/news/general-news/tragedy-behind-killing-fields-star-867613)

30. Bruce Lee

Bruce Lee. "Bruce Lee." (brucelee.com/bruce-lee, accessed Nov. 1, 2020)

Google Arts & Culture. "Bruce Lee." (artsandculture.google.com/entity/bruce-lee/ m099d4?hl=en, accessed Nov. 29, 2020)

Nittle, Nadra. "ESPN's Bruce Lee '30 for 30,' 'Be Water,' Shows How Much Racism Stole from Him and Audience." NBC News. June 7, 2020. (www.nbcnews.com/think/ opinion/espn-s-bruce-lee-30-30-be-water-shows-how-ncna1226631)

31. Yo-Yo Ma

Pressman, Robin. "How Yo-Yo Ma Inspired the New Mr. Rogers Documentary." KUSC. June 28, 2018. (www.kusc.org/culture/staff-blog/mr-rogers-yo-yo-ma)

Steinberg, Martin. "Yo-Yo Ma on Intonation, Practice, and the Role of Music in Our Lives." *Strings Magazine*, Sept. 17, 2015. (stringsmagazine.com/cellist-yo-yo-ma-on-practice-intonation-and-the-role-of-music-in-our-lives)

Yo-Yo Ma. "Life & Music." (www.yo-yoma.com/about-2, accessed Mar. 23, 2021)

32. Maya Lin

Art21. "Maya Lin." (art21.org/artist/maya-lin, accessed Apr. 17, 2021)

Becoming American: The Chinese Experience. "Maya Lin Bio." PBS. (www.pbs.org/ becomingamerican/ap_pjourneys_bio5.html, accessed Apr. 12, 2021)

McHenry, Eric. "Maya Lin Changes the Landscape of the Art World." *University of Washington Magazine*, Mar. 2006. (magazine.washington.edu/feature/maya-lin-changes-the-landscape-of-the-art-world)

33. Kalpana Chawla

Lyndon B. Johnson Space Center. "Kalpana Chawla: Biographical Data." National Aeronautics and Space Administration. May 2004. (www.nasa.gov/sites/default/files/ atoms/files/chawla_kalpana.pdf)

National Air and Space Museum. "Dr. Kalpana Chawla." Smithsonian Institution. May 2004. (airandspace.si.edu/support/wall-of-honor/dr-kalpana-chawla)

National Geographic India. "How Kalpana Chawla Decided to Be an Astronaut." Oct. 7, 2020. Video, 1:14. (www.youtube.com/watch?v=t-wpyBYb_X8)

News18. "17 Years after Kalpana Chawla's Death, Her Father Opens Up about Her Dream." Oct. 11, 2020. (www.news18.com/news/buzz/17-years-after-kalpana-chawlas-death-her-father-opens-up-about-her-dream-2941149.html)

Space Center Houston. "Astronaut Friday: Kalpana Chawla." Nov. 22, 2019. (spacecenter.org/astronaut-friday-kalpana-chawla)

34. Kamala Harris

Demby, Gene. "Let's Talk about Kamala Harris." NPR. Oct. 14, 2020. (www.npr.org/2020/10/13/923369723/lets-talk-about-kamala-harris)

SFGate. "17 Things You May Not Know about Kamala Harris." Oct. 10, 2018. (www.sfgate.com/politics/slideshow/things-you-might-not-know-about-Kamala-Harris-186005.php)

White House. "Kamala Harris." (www.whitehouse.gov/administration/vice-president-harris, accessed Aug. 23, 2021)

35. Tammy Duckworth

Johnson, Rebecca. "Senator Tammy Duckworth on the Attack That Took Her Legs—and Having a Baby at 50." *Vogue*, Sept. 12, 2018. (www.vogue.com/article/tammy-duckworth-interview-vogue-october-2018-issue)

PBS NewsHour. "Sen. Duckworth Writes of Resiliency, Healing in Her Book That's a 'Love Letter' to America." Transcript. Mar. 31, 2021. (www.pbs.org/newshour/show/sen-duckworth-writes-of-resiliency-healing-in-her-book-thats-a-love-letter-to-america)

Tammy Duckworth for U.S. Senate. "Meet Tammy." (tammyduckworth.com, accessed Nov. 21, 2020)

U.S. Senator Tammy Duckworth of Illinois. "About Tammy." (www.duckworth.senate.gov/about-tammy/biography, accessed Mar. 12, 2021)

36. Jerry Yang

Forbes. "Jerry Yang." (www.forbes.com/profile/jerry-yang/?sh=1540e640468b, accessed Nov. 12, 2021)

Immigrant Learning Center. "Jerry Yang." (www.ilctr.org/entrepreneur-hof/jerry-yang, accessed Nov. 12, 2021)

National Museum of American History. "Jerry Yang and Akiko Yamazaki." Smithsonian Institution. (americanhistory.si.edu/family-voices/individuals/jerry-yang-and-akiko-yamazaki, accessed Oct. 11, 2020)

37. Kristi Yamaguchi

California Museum. "Kristi Yamaguchi." (www.californiamuseum.org/inductee/kristi-yamaguchi, accessed Nov. 6, 2020)

Heisman Trophy. "Kristi Yamaguchi." (www.heisman.com/humanitarians/kristi-yamaguchi, accessed Nov. 4, 2020)

Hersh, Phil. "Yamaguchi and Ito: They're Worlds Apart—Except on the Ice." *Chicago Tribune*, Feb. 7, 1992. (www.chicagotribune.com/news/ct-xpm-1992-02-07-9201120465-story.html)

38. Dwayne "the Rock" Johnson

Eells, Josh. "Dwayne Johnson: The Pain and the Passion That Fuel the Rock." *Rolling Stone*, Apr. 4, 2018. (www.rollingstone.com/movies/movie-features/dwayne-johnson-the-pain-and-the-passion-that-fuel-the-rock-630076)

NPR. "'The Rock' on His Own Troubled Youth." Transcript. Sept. 15, 2006. (www.npr.org/templates/story/story.php?storyId=6081164)

Seven Bucks Digital Studios. "Seven Bucks Moment: Dwayne 'The Rock' Johnson." Dec. 6, 2016. Video, 5:57. (www.youtube.com/watch?v=RjATMi9yNd0)

39. Channapha Khamvongsa

Garunay, Melanie. "Channapha Khamvongsa: After War, a New Legacy of Peace in Laos." White House. Sept. 7, 2016. (obamawhitehouse.archives.gov/blog/2016/09/07/

channapha-khamvongsa-after-war-new-legacy-peace-laos)

Khamvongsa, Channapha. "In Laos, Clinton's Chance to Undo Lethal Legacy." CNN. July 11, 2012. (www.cnn.com/2012/07/11/opinion/khamvongsa-laos/index.html)

McCourt School of Public Policy. "Channapha Khamvongsa Receives McCourt Distinguished Alumni Award." Georgetown University. Aug. 28, 2017. (mccourt .georgetown.edu/news/channapha-khamvongsa-receives-mccourt-distinguished -alumni-award)

40. Sunisa "Suni" Lee

Diaz, Jaclyn, and Bill Chappell. "Gymnast Sunisa Lee's Gold Medal Elates Her Hometown Hmong Community." NPR. July 29, 2021. (www.npr.org/sections/ tokyo-olympics-live-updates/2021/07/29/1022077328/as-gymnast-sunisa-lee-goes-for-gold-her-hometown-hmong-community-has-her-back)

Feildstadt, Elisha. "Suni Lee Won Gold for Her Community, Her Family and Herself." NBC News. July 30, 2021. (www.nbcnews.com/news/olympics/suni-lee-won-gold-her-hmong-community-her-family-herself-n1275403)

Igoe, Katherine J. "Who Is Sunisa 'Suni' Lee, the Olympic Gymnast on the Cusp of Becoming a Household Name?" *Marie Claire*, July 30, 2021. (www.marieclaire.com/ culture/a37169991/who-is-sunisa-lee-gymnast)

Acknowledgments from the author

My deepest gratitude to Ah Kong and Maeh Thuu, my grandparents who immigrated from China, Thailand, and Laos. To Mom, your light shines down on me daily. To my Sisa-at and Ware family, your support means the world. To Juanita, Teela, and Sheela, families are forever and so is my love for you.

Much gratitude to my editors Margaret Raymo, Ciera Burch, and Monica Perez. Thanks for your guiding light. Thanks to Megan Gendell, Erika West, and others at Versify and HarperCollins. Victo Ngai, your beautiful work has brought these pages to life.

This book wouldn't exist without the encouragement of my literary agent, Ann Leslie Tuttle. Thank you for igniting the spark. My appreciation to all those at Dystel, Goderich & Bourret.

I've been fortunate to be part of many writing communities. All hail the Daily Universe, Neon Scribblers, SCBWI, Storymakers, DWENT, the Writers of the Lost Arc, and the Vermont College of Fine Arts. Special recognition to my mentors, Kaylene Armstrong, Robb Hicken, Linda Urban, Kekla Magoon, Cynthia Leitich Smith, Jane Kurtz, and David Gill.

To my friends who write, thank you for inspiring me: Annie Reynolds, Lindsey Leavitt, Erin Summerill, Ally Condie, Emily King, Emily Wing Smith, Julie Olson, Ann Dee Ellis, Axie Oh, and Erin Bay. Yamile Saied Méndez, you are a star.

Tamra and Evan, thank you for the library and love for this downstairs crew. Sunday night dinners always. Norma, you are my favorite neighbor. Erin, my favorite teacher.

Last, and never least, to those who hold my entire heart: the Awesome Bybees. My husband and best friend, Brendan, and my brightest lights: Mei, Cassius, Grey, and Selah. To all readers, may you find inspiration in the stories of these Asian Americans and Pacific Islanders as well as in your own.

Veeda Bybee

Acknowledgments from the artist

The manuscript of this book landed on my desk in April 2021, after months of regular anti-Asian attacks since the outbreak of COVID-19. I remember the week being particularly difficult because my husband had endured racial harassment in our neighborhood. I was feeling helpless about the situation and was especially worried about the future of our then five-month-old son. The opportunity of working on this book made me see a faint light of hope, one that I could contribute to and make brighter. Thank you, Veeda Bybee and HarperCollins, for having me and empowering me.

Thank you to my parents and to the trailblazers in this book and beyond for fighting the fight so that I can have the rights, platforms, and opportunities I enjoy, often without a second thought. Thank you to my husband, Yao, a self-proclaimed fan of strong women, who put up with my pre-deadline stress syndromes and inspires me daily. Thank you to my agent, Gail Gaynin, the best business partner one can ask for, a friend, a role model, and a part-time therapist. Thank you to my art directors, Samira Iravani and Alison Klapthor, for all your guidance, encouragement, and understanding through this project.

To my son, Day, this book is for you.

Victo Ngai